ADVANCE PRAISE

"This fast-moving, enjoyable book shows you how to be a happy, busy, self-fulfilled person – in every area of your life."

Brian Tracy
International Bestselling Author, Author – Maximum Achievement

"If anyone has insights into being happy, it's Shadé."

Adam Spencer
Author, Comedian & Former Triple J Radio Presenter

"WARNING: this is not your typical cheesy, preachy how-to book. It's so much more. Shadé has created a remarkably simple, insightful book that is delightfully different, infused with humor, sensitivity, warmth and a great deal of value. If you care about your relationships and want to be more successful in work and life, put this book on your required reading list."

Dr Ginni Mansberg
GP, Channel 7 TV Presenter & Author

"Shadé has written a simple, easy to read book around the key concepts of positive psychology. Full of personal anecdotes and stories, it covers the basics that we need to put into practice to deliver a happier, more fulfilling life. She brings critical research to life in a fun and engaging way, helping you realize that happiness is your choice - you are the architect! Thanks for this delightful contribution Shadé."

Sue Langley
Neuroscience Expert & CEO of Langley Group

"The path to living a successful and happy life is spelled out here in this book. Shadé makes the complexity of creating a fulfilling life very simple by using science, wisdom and her own personal stories. This is a must read for anyone who wants to take charge of their life to live abundantly and happily."

Tom Cronin
Founder of The Stillness Project, Speaker & Writer

"This book will transform how you think. More importantly, it will transform your life. A revelation."

Andy Bounds
Award Winning Sales Expert & Best Selling Author

"Shade stylistically guides us through utilizing effective ideologies, methods, anecdotes and research, toward becoming the decider, the architect and the captain of your life. A Fantastic and important book to read no doubt!"

Jack Delosa
Founder & CEO of The Entourage (BRW Young Rich List since 2014)

"A wonderful book! Through her enchanting personal experiences and powerful enablers, let Shadé steer you to become the Architect of your life!"

Mark D'Silva
Author of 'Zing! Speak like a Leader

"One could say that we already have enough books advising us how to be happy. But one could also argue that there's always room for another one if it offers a new and different approach. Shadé's contribution is certainly interesting and fresh; and I very much hope it helps more people to enjoy happiness and a good life."

Dr. Tim Sharp (aka. Dr. Happy)
International Leader in Positive Psychology, Speaker & Founder of The Happiness Institute

"In this warm and engaging book Shadé demonstrates that happiness is a choice and shares simple yet effective ways to make this choice. It's skillfully written with a rare mix of wisdom, fun and proven research, offering you an easy guide to lead a happier, more fulfilling life - and the graphics will keep you engaged to the end!"

Stacey Copas
Australia's #1 Keynote Speaker on Resilience & Author of 'How To Be Resilient

THE ART AND SCIENCE BEHIND DEVELOPING
ONE OF LIFE'S MOST IMPORTANT SKILLS
IN 5 SIMPLE HACKS!

I DON'T
WANT TO BE
HAPPY

- SAID NO ONE, EVER!

BY SHADÉ ZAHRAI

INFLUENCEO
GROUP PTY. LTD. Publishing

Published by Influenceo Group Pty. Ltd.
Sydney, Australia

influenceo.com.au

ISBN
978-0-6482261-0-9 (Paperback – Color)
978-0-6482261-2-3 (Paperback – Black & White)
978-0-6482261-1-6 (eBook)

Illustrations and book design by Justin Oefelein

"I want you
to be Happy…
to Laugh,
Smile and Rejoice
in order that others
may be made
Happy by you."

– 'Abdu'l-Bahá

CONTENTS

PREFACE

"Success is not the key to happiness.
Happiness is the key to Success."

\- Albert Schweitzer

So, you're probably thinking: ***"Why is happiness so important?"*** It's a very good question, especially since I'm the one who believes in it so much that I decided to write a book on it. It's important because, quite simply, it's the center of everything. It determines so much. It is the cause of so much. And, we are the ones who decide whether it plays a role in our lives or not. We are the ones who choose. But, it seems that so many have forgotten this simple fact.

There are two things I've noticed in our world. The first is that it seems that people everywhere are unhappy. They're miserable. They're going to jobs they dislike, doing work they despise, wondering why their success at work hasn't brought the happiness they thought it would, or maybe they are so miserable they aren't achieving any kind of success at all. They rarely get quality time with family and loved ones, have strained relationships as a result and are left questioning, ***"Is this it?"*** Heck, I was even wondering this some time ago as I sat on the train to work, surrounded by the 'corporate sardines' (it's always packed on my train line..). It's no way to live.

My second observation is that people have become despondent. They've given up. They've become like passengers in their lives, feeling like they're just along for the ride. No drive. No motivation. No momentum. Day in and day out, it's the same thing. **Wake up - Eat - Go to Work - Do the Work - Come Home - Dinner - Sleep.** And the next day? Repeat.

It doesn't help that we have developed an obsession with always being attached to our smart phones, our iPads and our laptops. We now live in a world where we're 'always-on'. Always connected. Always accessible. Always distracted. Email. Twitter. Instagram. Facebook. It's all-pervasive and it's becoming increasingly more difficult to escape from its all-encompassing grip. Just look around next time you're on public transport – I guarantee most people will be totally consumed in their device. As a result of 'stimulation overload', we've also developed somewhat of an attention deficit challenge… we basically have the attention spans of goldfish thanks to the ability to tap and swipe our way to something more interesting online.

PRETTY BLEAK OUTLOOK IF YOU ASK ME.

So, I wanted to do something about it. People needed to get a metaphorical 'kick up the backside' to realize that they had given away all of their power. They had succumbed to the evil grip of society, of comparing themselves to others and being miserable. Unfulfilled. Unsatisfied. Unhappy.

My desire for this book is to provide a glimpse into how easy it is to transform your life. Seriously, it's remarkably simple! But first, you need an understanding of the basics of Neuroscience and psychology and how it applies to our brains. Once you get this part, it makes it all seem so much easier. Trust me on this.

I Don't Want to Be Happy – said no one ever! invites you to explore the science behind how to transform your mind and life for the better. It aims to teach you how to train your mind and heart towards greater happiness and wellbeing in your daily life. It all starts with your thoughts. And, because I know you would probably get bored by page 3 if it didn't capture your attention in some engaging way, I've designed it so it's full of graphics to keep your brain at attention. Not too heavy but enough to satiate your curiosity. It's fresh, snappy, covers the key points that you need to kick-start your transformation and is super practical. No excuses now.

Your greatest and most precious resource is, without any shred of a doubt, your mind. Just as you'd go to the gym to keep your physical body in top condition, you should also be exploring ways to keep your mind in the best possible condition. Why? Well because (as some of you can surely relate) your mind can be the source of immense trauma, emotional baggage, or the darkest depression. Or, it can be a light – a source of positive energy, of motivation, of joy. When in this state, it becomes a resource for your deepest and most lasting happiness, which leads to greater fulfillment, life satisfaction and *(wait for it…)* success. It improves the quality of your relationships, changes your perspective and helps you continually grow and develop.

"BEING HAPPY IS NOT SOMETHING YOU <u>ARE</u>, IT'S SOMETHING YOU <u>DO</u>."

Happiness is at the center of everything. It's the key to success. If I've learned one thing, it's that being happy is not something you are, it's something you **do**. It requires a certain consciousness, a level of self-awareness. It involves a way of thinking, feeling and acting that is aligned, and if you can master it – *which I absolutely believe you can* – you'll be able to master your life. But you first have to choose to make a change. Become the Architect of your Life. I invite you to embark on the journey of taking back control. It's your life – you design it how you want it to be. **It's now or never.**

INTRODUCTION

"Happiness in intelligent people
is the rarest thing I know."

- Ernest Hemingway

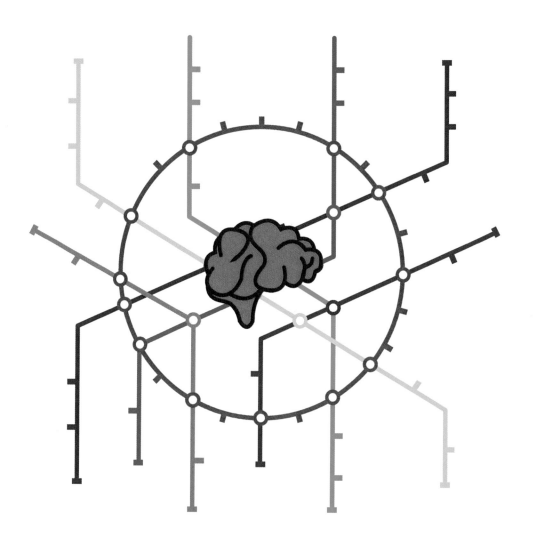

INTRODUCTION

Every good learning experience has it's beginning.
HERE'S MINE...

It was Tuesday morning. The weather was fresh, colder than usual given the time of year. I arrived at the train station a little later than normal (thanks to my love-hate relationship with my 'snooze' button), so I knew that the train would be packed. Making my way down the stairs to the platform, I yanked at my coat collar to protect my neck from the wind chill. I watched as the train pulled into the station, slowed to a stop and opened its doors. Crowds wedged through the door panels in search of the few remaining seats. Prime real estate.

I waited until everyone made their way through before I stepped onto the train, doors closing behind me with that familiar mechanical beeping rhythm. The train jolted to start as I scanned the carriage. There was one remaining seat within reach from where I stood. After a quick glance around to confirm it hadn't been 'visually claimed' by a fellow commuter, I squeezed through the crowd who seemed to pity me struggling with my oversized handbag, backpack and briefcase. Note to self: Start using the lockers at work.

YES, I GOT A SEAT!

Making eye contact with the lady I'd be sitting next to, I smiled, as if to seek her permission while simultaneously expressing my thanks, all in a single moment of silent communication. I had a tendency to do this – to break the isolation of 'passenger solitude' through a subtle attempt of communication: a fleeting moment of connection.

I slipped my handbag strap off my shoulder and removed my backpack then eased into the vinyl seat, placing both bags and my briefcase on my lap. Careful not to disturb my co-passenger, I fumbled with my personal items until I managed to pull my tangled headphones from my handbag. I connected the cable to my phone to play my morning soundtrack. I closed my eyes. The peace before the storm of the work day ahead.

You can imagine my surprise when that same lady who only FIVE MINUTES EARLIER had smiled back at me abruptly screamed,

"EXCUSE ME! Can you NOT let YOUR bag fall on ME?"

Woah, that was unexpected! Her furious eruption was harsh and loud enough to startle me over my music. I jolted to attention. Commuters as far as the end of the carriage stared in our direction, curious to make sense of the unprovoked outburst. I couldn't understand why she was so angry with me. She continued by mumbling obscenities, as if to make an even bigger scene. I removed my earphones. Confused, I stuttered, *"I'm…I'm so sorry…"* Glancing down, I removed the briefcase, which I only then realized had slipped from its place on my lap and was resting on her upper thigh. I lifted the briefcase and positioned it on the floor between my feet then shifted my gaze, staring blankly ahead of me, while she continued to mutter under her breath.

I felt so small. I knew this feeling. I'd been here before. *I'd felt this same way 23 years earlier when my 1ˢᵗ Grade teacher yelled at me in front of my classmates for emptying a bucket of pencils and wearing it on my head. I thought it made a fantastic hat, but it seemed that creativity and innovation were not celebrated in that class.* This moment, being 'told off' in front of a carriage of strangers, made me feel like I was six again. My stomach knotted. I felt humiliation creep over me, a mild feeling of nausea building in my gut.

My body slumped. I felt a weird combination of shame and numbness.

OK, you may be thinking "What's the big deal here? A random lady lost it on the train. It happens." While I'm the first to admit that I'm super sensitive to being the cause of upsetting others, I promise you – there's a point to the story.

The train slowed and then pulled to a stop at my station after what felt like a lifetime of trying to be as inconspicuous as possible. I stood from my place, grabbing my three bags. I turned to the lady next to me, unsure of what I would say. Once our eyes met (and hers were still enraged), I did something that surprised me. I smiled, a truly warm, genuine smile, one that originated from deep within.

With a sudden onset of newfound confidence, I gently and sincerely said,

> **"I'm so sorry again...**
> **It was completely unintentional.**
> **I hope you have a wonderful day."**

She gazed blankly at me, a perplexed expression washing over her harsh features. Before she had time to process, I turned around, still smiling, and made my way off the train towards my office.

I was still smiling the whole way to work.

> **"No one can make you feel inferior without your consent."**
>
> – Eleanor Roosevelt

I reflected on how this encounter had made me feel. I thought about how this complete stranger's actions had caused me to feel so insignificant, so 'in the wrong', for something that was entirely accidental and could have been resolved so effortlessly. Her abrupt tone, the harshness of her words, her insensitive approach: these all made me feel inferior to her and everyone else on that carriage. What I had done in that moment was to give her actions power over me. I allowed her words and tone to influence me, to make me feel a certain way.

11

At the time, I wasn't consciously aware of why I had chosen to smile at her and why I chose to continue smiling on my way to the office. This wasn't a smile to simply appear as the 'bigger person'. This smile was genuine. I 'felt' it. I meant it. It's only now on reflection that I know why it happened.

I didn't do it so much for her. Or perhaps I did. But I certainly did it for me. There was a moment when I was preparing to leave that I made a conscious decision to regain control of my emotions; to take back control of how I felt. I took a deep breath, took a moment to be present and straightened my posture. As a result, I suddenly and remarkably felt more confident, more at ease. Happier. More positive. Naturally, I wanted to share some of my positivity with her.

So as I walked to work, I began to think about how it would've been so easy for me to make a judgment about this lady, this stranger I really knew nothing about. Apart from a fleeting interaction, which, by all standards, was disappointing, I was in absolutely no position to judge her, her words or her actions. I could have easily concluded that she was just a rude, inconsiderate and self-centered person who didn't care about anyone else. Interestingly, most of us have a tendency to do this in our lives. We have a single negative interaction with another person and from their language used, the words shared or their expressions, we make all sorts of fundamental judgments about this person's character and personality.

This is such a common phenomenon that social psychologists have called it

FUNDAMENTAL ATTRIBUTION ERROR.

This happens when you judge that someone's behavior is a reflection of their personality and underestimate the possible influence of external factors.

On the train, I was in a position where I could have allowed this to happen. I could have both allowed my personal power to be stripped from me by this stranger as well as misjudged her as simply a narcissist. Neither of these would have helped me and how I was feeling.

In all honesty, I didn't know anything about this lady. I didn't know about her childhood, her family life, where she was going that morning or what had happened to her shortly before taking my seat. I didn't even know what she might have experienced immediately prior to her harsh words because I was focused entirely on my music. Maybe she had an injury on her thigh that was being aggravated by my briefcase. Maybe she had just heard some unfortunate news, and I just happened to be in the wrong place at the wrong time. I'll never know.

What I do know is this – at that moment I had a choice to make. I could've easily chosen to judge her. I could've allowed her tone to make me feel insignificant, as though I didn't matter. And that would've surely ruined my day.

> **"We are products of our past, but we don't have to be prisoners of it."**
>
> **– Rick Warren**

Instead, I chose to rise above all of it. I chose not to judge, and not to make assumptions.

I shifted my focus to my breathing and being aware of what I was feeling with the intention of redefining my emotions. I centered my focus only on myself. I redirected my thoughts to something positive and managed to convince myself that I had no reason not to be happy. That I was confident. That I was strong. This positivity gave me the strength and desire to share some of it with her. It seemed that she could also use it.

Who knows… maybe my kind words before I left made her feel better about her situation. Maybe my positive parting sentiment shifted something inside her. Again, I'll never know. But, thinking this way helped me overcome the situation. It helped me be bigger. Better. Stronger.

This experience, years ago now, marked a turning point in my journey of self-learning. It made me realize that we have absolutely no control over other people's thoughts, feelings or actions. The only thing that we have control over is ourselves. How we choose to interpret the world and respond to it is entirely up to us. While our perception of what happens in the world around us will be influenced by our previous experiences (and our inherent bias, values and perceptions), we have more control over ourselves and our future than we realize.

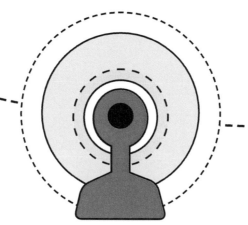

What is your life centered on?

In the world that we live in, we are surrounded by things screaming for our attention: the pull of social media, the pursuit of keeping up with the 'Kardashians', the next trending Netflix series, the excesses of consumerism... These all have an impact on how much time we spend investing in ourselves, in our own self-reflection and self-development. So many people I know define themselves entirely by what they have or what they do. I have colleagues who gain their life satisfaction from their jobs; from the new promotion they secured and the flashy new company car they were rewarded with. Their careers give their lives meaning.

Others I know are entirely focused on their social-media personas, concerned only with how they're perceived by their social-networks and how they measure in comparison with others. They spend their lives designing their online-presence, posting and liking, sharing and tweeting, gaining their sense of self-worth from other people's perceptions of them. A friend of mine removed a photo she had posted on social media because it hadn't received enough 'likes' in the first ten minutes.

These people have chosen to center their lives on factors external to themselves, always seeking validation and fleeting approvals from others and the instant gratification. However, where we find happiness in something external to ourselves it is only ever temporary.

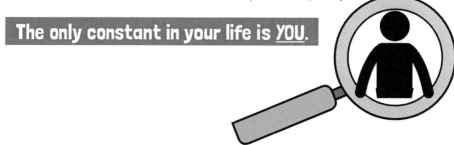

The only constant in your life is YOU.

The term 'self-centered' carries with it negative connotations around self-absorption, selfishness and narcissism. This isn't what I mean. What I DO MEAN is that we need to become more centered on ourselves, on who we are, how we got here, how we can improve ourselves in every way and what we need to do to be better people and more valuable contributors to society.

By focusing on ourselves, we avoid living life on autopilot. By becoming centered on Self, <u>it doesn't mean feeding our Ego</u>. It means engaging in daily reflection and self-assessment as a conscious process of self-refinement. It involves a "twin process" of focusing on Self, and focusing on how our Self can contribute to the needs of those around us. This includes our social environments, and building healthier and more fulfilling relationships.

Your career can easily come to an end. Your 'cyber' persona could all too easily be tarnished. You could lose all of your Instagram followers in a day. Instead of basing your sense of self-worth on something or someone that is inherently temporary and external to yourself, you should center your life on yourself – and what is true to you.

When we become centered on Self, we focus on becoming more confident, more grounded, more resilient and more in tune with who we are.

Audrey Hepburn once wrote,

'As you grow older, you discover you have two hands:

One for helping YOURSELF,

THE OTHER FOR HELPING OTHERS.'

The harsh reality is that if we don't look after ourselves first, no one else will do it for us. If we don't make sure that we're in control of our lives, we won't be able to help others. We must center on Self to the extent that we commit to being the best person we can and gain our sense of self-worth from within.

This book is a gift to all of those people whose paths I've crossed who have shared with me that they too are on their own journey of self-development and self-discovery. They, too, want to be centered on Self – as very distinct from ego. It seems that almost everyone I've spoken with wants to be better and is searching for the tools to help them get there. I've found – at least at this early stage of my journey – that by simply understanding a few simple concepts, and not denying that we should all be centered on Self, **we can choose to be the Architects of our Future.**

Believe in yourself.

Trust yourself.

Invest in yourself.

CHAPTER ONE

HOUSTON,
we have a problem

CHAPTER ONE

HOUSTON, we have a problem

'THE WORLD DOESN'T REVOLVE AROUND YOU.'

Actually, yes it does.

The world is full of remarkable people, leading remarkable lives and doing remarkable things. We pass these people each and every day - on the street, in the cafe and at work. Yet, so many of us, entirely consumed in our selfish thoughts in our lives, miss the opportunity to connect. Connecting with someone else could be as simple as sharing a smile, wishing someone well on their day, holding a door open for someone or simply asking,

'How are you today?' and actually meaning it.

Recently I sat next to an elderly man on an early morning flight from Sydney to Perth. When I identified which seat was mine, I made eye contact, smiled and said 'hello' as a warm introduction to my co-flier for the next four hours of my life. His response wasn't anything notable. A small gesture of return and the raising of an eyebrow in acknowledgment.

I crammed my backpack and jacket in the overhead locker and fumbled with my handbag, scarf, headphones, e-Reader, charger and water bottle, careful not to allow any items to accidentally spill out onto his seat – lesson learned from last time. When I finally buckled myself in and had all my belongings in order, I pulled out my phone to switch it to airplane mode.

While doing so, I noticed a handful of small toffee candies that I had taken the previous day from a family lunch at a local restaurant - the complimentary kind you are offered at a cashier.

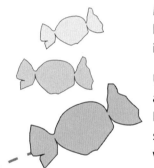

My family wasn't big on candy, but I happily helped myself to the lot and tossed them into my bag.

Underwhelmed by my initial brief interaction and lack of connection with 'Mr Eyebrow-Raise', I picked up one of the wrapped sweets, its red plastic wrapper crackling with my touch, and offered it to him.

'Would you like something sweet for take-off?'

He chuckled, displaying his joyous, hearty smile.

'Yes, please!'

'NEVER TOO EARLY FOR SOMETHING SWEET,' I REPLIED.

He commented how convenient it was to have a candy for take-off to assist with altitude effects:

> **'I find that my old ears don't handle the change in altitude like they used to.'**

This simple act of connection, of bridging a gap, prefaced a whole discussion about who we were. What are we doing? Where are we going? What is important to us? He shared how he had spent many years devoting himself to his career as a financial planner, working for a high-profile media mogul and traveling first-class around the world. He stated that, unlike many other financial planners he knew and worked with, he happened to be very good at taking his own advice and had set himself up with a very comfortable retirement. He was on his fourth visit to Perth this year to catch up with old friends and next week would be traveling to Europe to his holiday home in Bologna, looking forward to having four months to take his new toy, a shiny Harley Davidson, out for a spin. We shared our views on the importance of good leadership within organizations, the value of personal development and growth, and the simple joys of the finer things in life like good food, a good book and good company.

All this from the offer of a single candy...

WHEN AN EYEBROW-RAISE JUST DIDN'T FEEL RIGHT.

Had I not taken the step to address what I felt was an unsatisfactory introduction, the above scenario could have played out as follows.

Today I sat next to an elderly man on an early morning flight from Sydney to Perth. We took off. We landed. I left.

Uneventful, unmemorable, NORMAL.

So often, we allow ourselves to fall into the pattern of 'normal'. Of course, the question 'what is normal?' is entirely debatable. But for the purposes of the point I'm making here, 'normal' is simply how I put it before – uneventful, unmemorable, 'the norm'. We go through much of our lives content with this way of doing things. Content with being under-stimulated, too consumed by the noise of our own thoughts to engage with the world around us.

Yet by doing this, we are depriving ourselves of the joy that comes from connecting with others. We self-sabotage the potential joy of meeting and interacting with an absolute stranger, sharing a moment, learning about their lives, their life lessons, their struggles, and feeding the sapling of human connection within us that is nourished each time we share a smile with a stranger.

But how can we be open to others when we're still battling with ourselves? And how can we be present when we're still trying to understand why we react to things the way we do? Why do we feel the things we feel? Why is it that so much of 'us' is still unpredictable? This is simply because we haven't taken the time to invest in ourselves. We don't take moments to reflect on 'us', to equip ourselves with an understanding of what drives us and shapes our experience of the world.

There are certain human truths I believe all of us should be aware of: the basics, the fundamentals, the precursor to being our best selves, being content with who we are and feeling like we are in control of our future. This all hinges on an understanding of the mind and the mental and cognitive resources we have available to us.

LET'S EXPLORE

CHAPTER TWO

Run Towards a
SOLUTION

Run Towards a SOLUTION

WHAT LIES BENEATH: WELCOME TO THE SUBCONSCIOUS

I've never been a big advocate for 'New Year's resolutions', as I question why a resolution can't be made any time of the year. But – despite that – I still do find myself looking forward to December 31 each year because I find the opportunity to review everything I *didn't* do. I'm able to reassess what I want to achieve in the coming year and make a commitment to change. Last year, I made a resolution to invest in 'me' and take one Yoga class per week. Not a huge commitment, but one I felt was realistic and practical. I was excited to have allocated time in my weekly schedule to dedicate to centering myself. January 1 came around and I eagerly purchased an online ten-week pass at my local studio; it arrived via email two-minutes later.

How many times did I go to yoga class that year?

ZERO.

Did I even print off the online pass?

NO.

Why? It's quite simple, and it all comes down to the mind.

When most people think of the mind, they think of what's called the 'conscious mind'.

The conscious mind is the objective, thinking mind that we engage to think about the world, to imagine and to set goals in our lives. The conscious mind is your awareness of the present moment. It's what you have voluntary control over, so naturally, it's what many people consider to be the 'whole' mind.

Have you ever made a New Year's resolution, like I did, and then broken it? If so, never fear. You're not lacking in self-control or devoid of willpower. According to research, you're just like the majority of people who commit to a New Year's resolution and don't stick to it.

When we make a resolution, we engage our conscious mind to set goals for the coming year. The reason why these New Year's resolutions are rarely maintained is simple – it's because the mind is like an iceberg. You don't have to have seen *The Titanic* to know that only 10% of an iceberg can be seen from above the water's surface.

While you only have one mind, it possesses two distinct and characteristic functional components. The two functions of the mind are essentially different to each other, and each plays a different role. Just like the portion of an iceberg that you can see, we only use our conscious mind 10% of the time. The other 90% of our mind falls in the realm of the Subconscious, and this is what has control over our thoughts, feelings and actions the vast majority of the time. This is why I never used the yoga pass; my conscious mind thought that by committing to the purchase, I'd go to the class. My Subconscious resisted the "change" in routine and wanted to preserve what it was comfortable with – which was doing nothing.

Despite how significant our Subconscious is in terms of its influence on how we perceive the world around us, most people don't really understand how it works. There is also very little recognition of the power we have over it.

You are the architect of your life and the master of your fate. Remember, you have the luxury of choice.

CHOOSE TO TAKE CONTROL.

CHOOSE TO BE POSITIVE.

CHOOSE TO BE HAPPY.

"Folks are usually about as happy as they make their minds up to be."

- Abraham Lincoln

CHAPTER THREE

Self-REFINE

CHAPTER THREE

Self-REFINE

William James, the father of American psychology, said,

'OUR GREATEST TREASURE IS THAT WHICH IS HIDDEN DEEP WITHIN OUR OWN SUBCONSCIOUS'.

There are actually countless cognitive and psychological resources available to help us tap into our Subconscious and gear us towards greater happiness (Yay!). Many of these fall within the realm of Positive Psychology, a relatively new branch of psychology that moves away from the traditional deficit model by shifting focus away from what's clinically 'wrong'. Instead, the focus is on the promotion of wellbeing and the creation of greater happiness. By focusing on creating a life that's filled with meaning and accomplishment and is fulfilling and flourishing, we can rewire our brains and 'turn our faces to the sunshine'.

Happiness is a choice. It's a state of mind. A habit. It's a conscious decision to think, say and do things that are aligned, and when repeated regularly, these systematically sink into the Subconscious. **After sifting through research from Neuroscience and leading positive psychology researchers, I've narrowed the science down to just five easy life hacks. I believe these are universal working basics to greater happiness, confidence and success – that <u>will</u> transform your life.**

These hacks aren't rocket science, and you don't need to acquire any special powers to allow yourself to tap into your Subconscious. You already have the power you need. But, just like any latent capability, you do have to learn how to use these 'powers'. You have to first understand it so that you can apply it in all aspects of your life. Sometimes it's the simplest of things that can have the greatest impact.

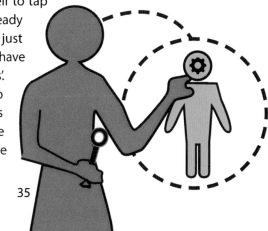

35

FIVE HACKS

i.   As we Think, So we Become

THE POWER OF POSITIVE THINKING

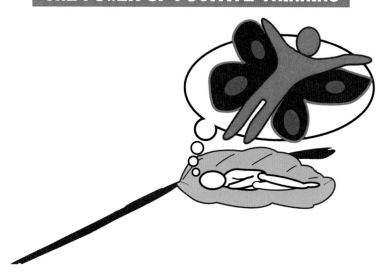

ii.   Take the Shackles off my feet

SELF– LIMITING BELIEFS

iii. Little Thing, Big Difference

ATTITUDE

iv. Just Because

GRATITUDE

v. Be the Change

HELP OTHERS & MAKE A DIFFERENCE

HACK
1. AS WE THINK, SO WE BECOME

> "If you tell yourself something often enough
> **YOU WILL START TO BELIEVE IT..."**
> **– Leon Brown**

Positive psychology research overwhelmingly suggests that the more frequently we repeat positive statements of self-belief, confidence and hope, the happier we feel. These positive affirmations about our abilities can, through continuous repetition, become imprinted on our subconscious mind. It's as though **we become what we think about most.** The same thing applies to the negative – if we constantly *think* in a negative, self-defeating way about our lives, we naturally start to *live* in a self-defeating way. We begin to think that we're trapped and doomed to fail or live a life of mediocrity because there's no way around it. This mindset makes us miss opportunities and the beauty of life, and this 'opportunity-blindness' acts to reinforce this initial negativity.

On the other hand, the use of positive affirmations – *the repetition of personal, positive present-tense statements* – helps the Subconscious reprogram itself. These statements have the power to override negative beliefs or thoughts that are already deeply ingrained in the Subconscious as a result of prior experience or insecurities.

Think about a vinyl record (remember those?) that has various tracks imprinted in it. Now imagine that the more frequently a track is played, the deeper the imprint becomes and the louder it plays. These tracks are just like the neural pathways within your brain. The repetition of positive affirmations fundamentally shifts your attitude while creating stronger neural pathways (just like deeper grooves in the record). Affirmations also help the Subconscious to start 'acting' in those ways to bring the new affirmations into reality. For example, the simple repetition of the words *"I choose to be happy no matter what"* can alter your mindset about anger, disappointment, negativity or sadness.

SEE IT IN YOUR MIND:
Making it happen with
VISUALIZATION

When I was in school, my mother always used

to say, "Visualize what you want!

Do you see it? Can you feel it?"

To this I would always respond with "YES, MOM."

Truth is, I really didn't see it. I couldn't feel anything.
I didn't understand what benefit that would give me.
Little did I know, at the time, that she was onto a good thing.

THE COGNITIVE TECHNIQUE OF VISUALIZATION, also known as Mental Imagery or Visual Mental Rehearsal, is used by key innovators and idea generators at some of the most creative companies of the world. It's commonly used by start-ups when designing and creating new products, it aids the creative process, allows for 'blue sky thinking' and taps into that area of the brain that we've been discussing: the Subconscious.

Visualization has been proven to be extraordinarily successful in producing specific results. It's a game changer.

AH, NOW I GET IT – sorry for doubting you, Mother!

Research suggests that our Subconscious plays an important role in shaping how we experience the world. This means that it may be possible to program our mind and body to respond in a certain way to gain a desired outcome.

Here is a fascinating fact:

The Subconscious has no ability to differentiate

BETWEEN WHAT'S REAL AND WHAT'S IMAGINED.

By visualizing positive outcomes, we expose our Subconscious to a desirable future that hasn't occurred yet. This then enables both our mind and body to become responsive and conditioned to that desired result. It works like this – our bodies are primed to respond physiologically to what we experience, and when we visualize a positive outcome it actually has a positive effect on our biochemistry. The mind comes to believe that what you're visualizing has already been achieved and therefore primes us to make it our reality.

Think back to the last time you watched a horror movie. Do you remember how your body responded? Did you notice the palms of your hands become sweaty? Did you notice your heart rate increase? Perhaps you flinched when something caught you by surprise?

Now that you understand at least a little about the Subconscious, it's easy to understand why your body responds like this. *Your Subconscious responds to whatever it's exposed to.* Your body is primed to respond physiologically to what you see. When you're engrossed in a movie, your Subconscious **cannot tell the difference between whether its a real experience or make believe!**

When you watched the horror movie, you weren't in any real physical danger, but your Subconscious absorbed what was on the screen and assumed you were facing a real threat. As a result, the amygdala in the limbic part of your brain became activated – this is the emotion center responsible for the 'fight or flight' response. Your brain registered the negative emotion of fear. Your adrenal glands would have released cortisol and your sensory awareness would have been heightened. Your brain and body were priming you to escape: the survival instinct.

Just like how we undergo involuntary physiological changes in response to what we 'see' when we're watching a horror movie, we can also use this knowledge for our own benefit. We can simulate a positive scenario or desirable outcome in our minds by creating a positive mental image. It's a remarkable effortless style of thinking that you can choose to adopt in your everyday life to help bring about your desired reality – or at least a clearer picture as to how to reach it.

So, how do you do it? You need to take time to imagine what you want. See it in front of you – what it looks like, what it feels like, what it smells like and what it sounds like. Whether it's winning a public speaking competition, being recognized for delivering outstanding work to your boss, or hiring your first employee at your newly established social enterprise – hold these images in your mind and make sure you associate these with positive emotions. When you create these positive mental images, you stimulate your Subconscious. By continually returning to these positive images you've visualized, you trigger a process where your Subconscious will accept them as reality and direct your behavior as needed towards achieving your desired goal.

This simple technique of visualization, when done right, can have a huge influence on your ability to achieve your goals and reaching your desired future.

This is sometimes known as **ONTOLOGICAL DESIGN:** the process by which you can shape your reality, and your reality then shapes your behavior, which further shapes your reality... and so the process continues.

What Positive Affirmations Do to Your Brain

According to renowned positive psychologist Barbara Fredrickson in her article *What Good Are Positive Emotions?* (1988), positive emotions and positive affirmations (and by default, visualization of positive and desirable outcomes) broaden your sense of possibility. They enhance your overall sense of self and improve your subjective wellbeing.

This concept was demonstrated in an experiment that tested the impact of positive emotions on the brain. Research participants were divided into five groups and each group was shown different film clips that were designed to evoke differing emotions.

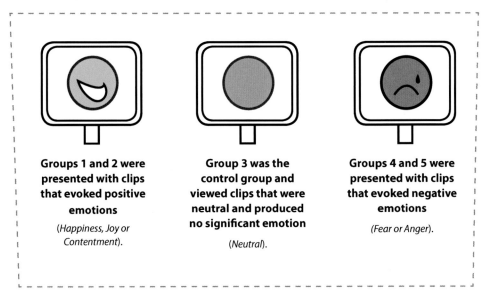

Groups 1 and 2 were presented with clips that evoked positive emotions

(Happiness, Joy or Contentment).

Group 3 was the control group and viewed clips that were neutral and produced no significant emotion

(Neutral).

Groups 4 and 5 were presented with clips that evoked negative emotions

(Fear or Anger).

After viewing their allocated film clips, each participant was asked to imagine themselves in a situation where they'd experienced similar feelings. They were then asked to write down what they would do. Each participant was handed a piece of paper with 20 blank lines that started with the phrase, *"I would like to..."*

Participants from Groups 4 and 5 who were presented with clips that evoked fear and anger (the negative emotional stimulus) wrote down the fewest responses. In comparison, the participants from Groups 1 and 2, who viewed clips of joy, happiness and contentment (the positive emotional stimulus), wrote down a significantly higher number of actions that they would take, even when compared with the neutral group.

This experiment highlights that when you experience positive emotions such as joy, happiness and contentment, even if only in response to a stimulus (like the film clips), you're able to identify and recognize more possibilities in your life. There are more options surrounding you, you feel that you have more choices available and you're more grateful for what you have. These findings were among the first to suggest that positive emotions broaden your sense of possibility – they open your mind to new perspectives, new ways of doing things and new ways of thinking.

IDEAS TO REMEMBER

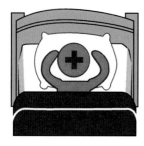

1. Prior to sleep (because research shows us that sleep consolidates memory), repeat a positive affirmation to your Subconscious and it will prove to you just how powerful repeated positive affirmations can be.

2. Imagine the happy ending or solution you're seeking, in all parts of your life. See it in your mind. What you imagine and feel will be accepted by your Subconscious, which will prime you to bring it to reality.

3. Remind yourself just how powerful your Subconscious mind is and how you can use its power to increase your confidence and overall wellbeing.

Challenge ONE

The Power Of Positive Thinking

POSITIVE AFFIRMATION

Think about three positive affirmations: self-loving statements about yourself. These could be focused on enhancing your self-esteem, specific to something you want to work on, or maybe you just want to think about affirmations that relate to a more positive attitude in general.

Here are some examples.
- *I choose to be happy by default at all times*
- *I can do anything I set my mind to*
- *I have infinite potential to succeed*

Write yours below and repeat them each night.

1. _____
   _____
   _____

2. _____
   _____
   _____

3. _____
   _____
   _____

HACK II. TAKE THE SHACKLES OFF MY FEET

Self-Limiting Beliefs

> "Whether you think you can, or you think you can't,
>
> **YOU'RE RIGHT."**

– Henry Ford

A ccording to research, the average person has approximately 60,000 thoughts per day. Believe it or not, over 80% of these thoughts are negative – negative comments about our abilities, negative self-talk and negative thoughts about the world. Given our understanding of the Subconscious, imagine the effect this has on our outlook and how we perceive and interpret the world around us.

Here's a fascinating finding about the influence of self-belief on performance. According to research into gender equality in schools from the Organization for Economic Co-operation and Development called The ABC of Gender Equality in Education (2015), school-aged girls lack self-confidence in solving maths and science problems. This lack of self-belief means they achieve worse results in these subjects, despite outperforming boys overall.

The research states that *"gender disparities in performance do not stem from innate differences in aptitude"* but rather from students' attitudes towards learning and the confidence they have in their abilities.

47

This actually blew my mind when I first came across it, because I realized how school-aged students' perceived lack of ability continues to influence the types of jobs and careers they would choose as they enter adulthood, shaping their future. It's a perfect example of the remarkable link between self-belief, behavior and choices throughout life.

Let's face it… we're all guilty of having fallen into a self-limiting mindset at some point in our lives. The narrative would play out like this: once-upon-a-time we had a negative experience (maybe in childhood or adolescence), and from that moment onwards we continued to re-live the story in our minds. This has allowed it to influence our thinking about what *might* and *could* go wrong the next time we're faced with a similar situation. We start to use limiting language such as 'I can't…', 'I'm not good at…' or 'It's too hard…'.

Our Subconscious then becomes fixated on this negative narrative, highlighting all the things that could limit us. Soon enough, through a behavioral feedback loop, our Subconscious accepts this as being true and begins to create it in our reality. You might have heard of this as a self-fulfilling prophecy – a prediction that directly or indirectly causes itself to become true due to positive feedback between belief and behavior.

You may have told yourself at one point or another that you're not capable of succeeding in a particular area no matter how focused you try to be. Perhaps you've never thought of yourself as a talented public speaker, and in fact become debilitated by nerves even at the thought of standing in front of a large audience. Simply the idea of it entering your mind has the effect of making your stomach churn or your heart-rate start to quicken.

As you repeat these self-limiting thoughts, they become impressed upon your Subconscious; you begin to have less confidence in these areas and increased self-doubt. This is how you self-sabotage. Before you even realize it on a conscious level, these beliefs have brought about the reality.

How do we self-limit?

According to the Mayo Clinic, a non-profit organization committed to clinical practice, education and research, there are four negative thought processes that limit our ability to succeed. We're sometimes not even aware of when we start to think in these ways and they can easily jeopardize our self-confidence and subjective-well-being. See which ones you may be able to relate to.

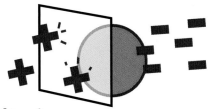

Filtering.

"I have so much to do and I'm so stressed... I'm going to fail."

Filtering is where you become fixated on all the negative aspects of an experience and magnify them, blowing them out of proportion. You basically filter out the positive.

You might fail to notice the compliment someone paid you at work, or maybe you forget about everything you should be grateful for in life. The source of negativity – whether it's a life stressor, something that's making you anxious or is causing you fear – becomes the only focus of your attention.

Personalizing.

*"It's all my fault.
I ruin everything I touch."*

If something negative happens, your automatic response is to blame yourself and to self-condemn. For example, you and your partner arrive late to a dinner party and the host burnt the turkey roast. You believe that you caused the ruined meal because you didn't push your partner to leave on time.

Polarizing.

"I couldn't even make it though my full gym workout this afternoon. I'm such a failure. I'm useless. There's no point in trying anymore."

You find yourself unable to silence your inner critic. You feel that you must be absolutely perfect and flawless in all aspects of your life, otherwise you're an utter failure. You essentially give up if you can't instantly achieve everything you want, or maybe your fear of failure holds you back from persisting and trying again.

Catastrophizing.

"I missed my alarm and now I'm already running late… Everything is going to go wrong today!"

Your automatic default is to expect the worst-case scenario. You miss your alarm one morning and you genuinely believe this is a sign that the rest of your day, regardless of what you have planned, will be nothing short of catastrophic. You tend to over-emphasize the negative and make things seem worse than they really are.

Do you have any self-limiting thoughts that pop into your mind when you wake up in the morning? The extent to which you think negative thoughts and allow limiting self-talk, especially when you start your day, has a huge influence how the day unfolds. If you have any of these four self-limiting thoughts first thing in the morning, you'll attract these experiences. Through the process of confirmation bias (the tendency to search for information that confirms your preconceptions), you'll have a heightened awareness to anything that supports your negative perception. Even where nothing exists, your brain will perceive things in such a way that your negative belief is confirmed. You're priming your Subconscious to focus on negativity; this makes you unhappy and limits your ability to succeed. It is self-sabotage.

The self-limiting thoughts perpetuate themselves as your Subconscious accepts them to be true and primes you to make them reality. As the great Roman philosopher Marcus Aurelius said, *'A man's life is what his thoughts make of it.'* This is why it's so important to have a heightened awareness of our thoughts, especially first thing in the morning.

IDEAS TO REMEMBER

1. Whatever your conscious mind assumes and believes will be embraced by your Subconscious – make sure you avoid any negative, defeatist or self-limiting thoughts.

2. Your Subconscious won't argue with you. If you tell yourself that you can't do something, your Subconscious accepts it to be true. You have the power to choose your thoughts and reject those that are negative and self-limiting.

3. Whenever your mind takes you to the place of *'I can't…',* overcome the fear and doubt by substituting the following:

   'I can do anything I put my mind to. If I don't achieve it the first time, I will keep trying and improving.'

2 Challenge TWO

Eliminating Limiting Language

Your Subconscious Mind accepts as true whatever you keep saying to it. With knowledge comes power, so here's where we make a commitment to put an end to self-limiting beliefs and negative self-talk.

Take a moment of silent reflection now to think about the last time you fell victim to self-limiting language. Think about what the negative beliefs were about and what unhelpful statements you would repeat to yourself. Write these down below.

Then, for every negative thought and limitation you wrote down on the left, think about a corresponding positive affirmation that will give you confidence to focus on your abilities and talents.

Once you've completed this, read through the positive affirmations on the right-hand side in your mind and really speak them with conviction. Visualize what they will look like in practice and how your behavior will align to bring them to reality. This is how we trigger our Subconscious to accept them as new standards of thought and behavior.

NEGATIVE SELF-LIMITING LANGUAGE	POSITIVE AFFIRMATION
Examples:	
I overcommit and can't get anything done.	I'm passionate and only commit to what I can get done to my best ability.
I'm too stubborn and can't change.	I am open minded to new perspectives and I have conviction in my values & beliefs.
1.	
2.	
3.	

HACK III.

LITTLE THING, BIG DIFFERENCE

Attitude

> "The greatest discovery of my generation is that a human being can alter his life by altering his attitude."
>
> — William James

What's your explanatory style?

Attitude is often understood in terms of explanatory style. Your explanatory style relates to the reasoning you use to explain why events happen – to yourself, to others and to the world. People with a positive attitude generally have an **OPTIMISTIC EXPLANATORY STYLE**. As the name suggests, these people seek out the positive in every situation, tend to give themselves credit when good things happen, and typically attribute bad outcomes to forces beyond their control. They also tend to see negative events as temporary and atypical. This makes them more resilient, more confident and better equipped to handle the inevitable challenges of life. Psychologist Carol Dweck refers to this as a 'growth mindset', one that recognizes opportunities to learn from every experience and that people can change if they choose to.

On the other hand, a **PESSIMISTIC EXPLANATORY STYLE** is one that frequently blames internal factors when bad things happen. In short, you engage in self-blame. If you have a pessimistic explanatory style, you'll more than likely fail to give yourself adequate credit for successful outcomes. You'll make excuses when good things happen and will doubt their re-occurrence. You have a tendency to view negative events as expected and ongoing. Naturally, this type of self-blaming for events outside the span of your control or viewing these unfortunate events as a persistent part of life can have a detrimentally negative and lasting impact on your state of mind, confidence, overall happiness and subjective wellbeing. This is often described as a **'fixed mindset'.**

One of the most eminent and influential psychologists on the topic of attitude is Martin Seligman. In his book *Learned Optimism* (1991), he states:

"The defining characteristic of **PESSIMISTS** is that they **tend to believe that bad events will last a long time,** will undermine everything they do, and are their own fault.

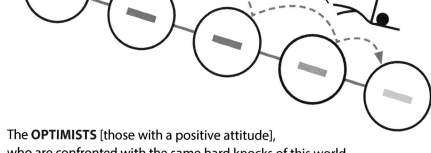

The **OPTIMISTS** [those with a positive attitude],
who are confronted with the same hard knocks of this world,
think about misfortune in the opposite way.

They tend to believe that defeat is just a temporary setback or a challenge, that its causes are just confined to this one case."

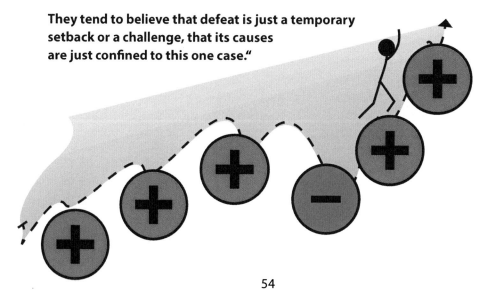

According to Seligman, a negative attitude activates a 'battle-stations' mode of thinking; you become focused solely on everything that's wrong and fixated on how to eliminate it (or wallow in your own self-pity when you decide that there's no solution). In contrast, a positive attitude prompts a way of thinking that's creative, tolerant, constructive, generous, non-defensive and accepting. It's even thought that a positive attitude results from activating a different part of the brain entirely.

The research indicates that if you have a more **optimistic explanatory style**, you're also more satisfied with your job and your work environment. You're more productive and on average have a higher income (go figure!). You're more likely to be noticed for promotion and have your work recognized. People tend to like you more, you have more friends and are more socially connected. These all contribute to making you more resilient to setbacks, more likely to try new things, and generally a happier person. Not a bad deal.

What is the relationship between
ATTITUDE AND HAPPINESS?

In another of his books, *Authentic Happiness* (2002), Seligman suggests a simple equation to help understand the degree of control we have over our happiness. If you're the type who likes formulas or simplified concepts, then you'll love this.

HERE GOES:

$$H = S + C + V$$

AND HERE'S WHAT EACH LETTER STANDS FOR:

is your enduring level of HAPPINESS

is your SET range

is the CIRCUMSTANCES of your life

represents factors under your VOLUNTARY control.

Enduring level of HAPPINESS

When Seligman speaks of an enduring level of happiness, he's not referring to momentary bursts of happiness, which could be triggered by a creamy white hot-chocolate on a cold winter's day or being first to purchase the latest tech gadget. These are temporary and short-lived. What he's referring to is your general overall sense of happiness.

This overall sense of happiness is made up of three components: your 'SET range' (S), the 'CIRCUMSTANCES of your life' (C) and 'factors under your VOLUNTARY Control' (V).

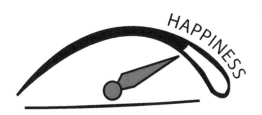

HERE'S A MIND BOGGLING FACT:

S

SET Range (Barrier to becoming happier)

If you were to sit a 'Happiness Indicator' test, about 50% of your score would be accounted for by your biological parents' score (this is also based on Lyubomirsky's work on the Happiness Pie).

Our 'set point' of happiness and positivity is largely genetically predetermined.

**What does this actually look like?
Ah, I'm glad that you asked... Here are 3 examples:**

1 In a study of lottery winners, after an initial spike in happiness, most people returned to their previous levels and styles of happiness within just twelve months.

2 People who become quadriplegic later in their life experience an initial period of depression; however, they usually recover their more-positive mood within a few months once they've come to terms with their new lifestyle.

3 The 'hedonic treadmill' is the tendency for people to return to their set levels of happiness irrespective of major positive or negative changes in their lives. It's often seen where people start taking things for granted in their lives. And they might even start seeking repeated instant gratification experiences, to keep re-boosting their levels of happiness. For example, continual holidays around the world or buying a new luxury sports car every year.

C

Life CIRCUMSTANCES

**This is self-explanatory -
The circumstances in which you live impact your overall levels of happiness.**

Circumstances like age, health, nationality, location of birth and the events we have experienced in childhood and adulthood can impact how we view the world and our mindset towards it.

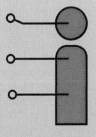

So which elements of Seligman's formula can we control? We can't control what life hands us and we don't have any ability to change our innate set range.

What we DO have voluntary control over is how we choose to perceive our lives and how we choose to explain the world around us.

What does that mean for our Subconscious mind?

The happiness equation tells us that our thoughts and actions are the only way that we can influence the overall happiness of our lives. But we also know that a vast majority of our thoughts originate from, and are created by our Subconscious. This raises the importance of using **CHOICE** to regain control of our attitudes. We can choose whether or not to use positive affirmations, whether or not to visualize and whether or not to remove `self-limiting' beliefs.

Your attitude influences your thoughts and feelings. Your thoughts and feelings influence your actions. Your actions determine how happy you are in your life. If we can commit to viewing everything through the lens of positivity and view the world through an optimistic explanatory style, nothing in life becomes too much trouble, and there is always time.

IDEAS TO REMEMBER

1. Newton's Third Law explains the physical relationship of action to reaction. If thought is 'action' then 'reaction' is the involuntary and automatic response of your Subconscious. So be aware of how your explanatory style shapes your perception of how the world responds back to you.

2. Adopting a pessimistic explanatory style means that you dwell on obstacles, delays and difficulties. Your Subconscious reacts by focusing entirely on the negative and which then influences your mood, confidence and ability to seek solutions. It serves you better to choose an optimistic explanatory style.

3. Life is not what happens to you, but how you choose to respond. You, and only you, are responsible for the way that you perceive, interpret and explain the world around you. Choose optimism. Choose happiness.

Attitude is Everything

Each letter's value corresponds to the number below it.

A	B	C	D	E	F	G	H	I	J	K	L	M	N	O	P	Q	R	S	T	U	V	W	X	Y	Z
1	2	3	4	5	6	7	8	9	10	11	12	13	14	15	16	17	18	19	20	21	22	23	24	25	26

IF HARD WORK

H	+	A	+	R	+	D	+	W	+	O	+	R	+	K	
8	+	1	+	18	+	4	+	23	+	15	+	18	+	11	= 98%

KNOWLEDGE

K	+	N	+	O	+	W	+	L	+	E	+	D	+	G	+	E	
11	+	14	+	15	+	23	+	12	+	5	+	4	+	7	+	5	= 96%

MONEY

M	+	O	+	N	+	E	+	Y	
13	+	15	+	14	+	5	+	25	= 72%

LEADERSHIP

L	+	E	+	A	+	D	+	E	+	R	+	S	+	H	+	I	+	P	
12	+	5	+	1	+	4	+	5	+	18	+	19	+	8	+	9	+	16	= 89%

A	+	T	+	T	+	I	+	T	+	U	+	D	+	E	
	+		+		+		+		+		+		+		= __%

Our ATTITUDE is what determines our happiness.
It is the only thing that we have complete voluntary control over.

60

HACK
IV. JUST BECAUSE

Gratitude

> "It's not happy people who are thankful.
> **IT'S THANKFUL PEOPLE WHO ARE HAPPY."**
> — Anon

This is a seemingly simple concept and it makes perfect sense once you understand the reasoning behind it. According to positive psychology researchers, one of the biggest factors contributing to overall happiness in your life is how grateful you are. Gratitude is the thankful appreciation for what a person receives, whether tangible or intangible. With gratitude, you acknowledge and remind yourself of all the good things in your life.

Gratitude is many things to many people: appreciation for what you have, being optimistic when faced with challenges, recognizing wonderful people in your life or 'counting your blessings'. One of the most wonderful things about gratitude is that it brings with it considerable physical and psychosocial effects. It helps you feel more positive emotions, reminds your Subconscious of all the great things in your life, improves your health, makes you more resilient to setbacks and challenges, makes you feel happier and helps you develop and nurture deep and enduring relationships.

Gratitude and Optimism

In a 2003 study on gratitude conducted by Emmons & McCullough three randomly assigned groups of participants were asked to keep a short journal each week. Each participant was given one of three tasks that they had to complete on a weekly basis.

61

- **GROUP 1** briefly described five things they were grateful for that had occurred in the past week.

- **GROUP 2** recorded daily hassles from the previous week that displeased them.

- **GROUP 3** (the neutral group) was asked to list five events or circumstances that affected them, but they were not told whether to focus on the positive or on the negative.

Ten weeks later, participants from Group 1, who described things they were grateful for on a weekly basis, had considerably more positive outcomes; they exercised more regularly, reported fewer physical symptoms, felt better about their lives as a whole, and were more optimistic about the upcoming week compared with Groups 2 and 3.

In another similar study, participants were asked to allocate time every day to write down things in their lives that they were grateful for. This daily practice of gratitude revealed some interesting results: participants who kept daily gratitude lists were more likely to have made progress toward important personal goals. *Who would've thought!*

They also reported offering others more emotional support or help with a personal problem. Not surprisingly, the gratitude exercise was shown not only to have profound individual benefits in terms of increasing goal achievement, but also enhanced a desire to help others (known as increasing 'pro-social' motivation).

Gratitude can be expressed in many ways. It can be past, present or future oriented.

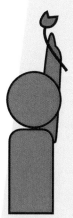

Gratitude about the PAST

You are who you are today because of everything you've been through. Your life journey is what has brought you to this point in time and space. You can express gratitude for your past, for every setback, for every obstacle and every challenge, and redefine them as events or circumstances that have helped you learn, grow and gain strength. Importantly, you can even choose to return to a negative memory and be thankful for the lesson it taught you. In this way, you learn to carry only gratitude for every experience in your childhood and every person who has crossed your path.

Gratitude about the PRESENT

How present you are on a daily basis affects how aware you are of all the good in your life. You should always be thankful for everything you have and mindful not to take anything for granted. So many of us find that we've placed expectations and sometimes impossible standards on ourselves, and we become fixated on what we don't have. It's an insatiable urge to seek the unattainable. Instead, we should reflect on where we are now and focus our attention to everything we do have.

Gratitude about the FUTURE

Many people are fearful of the future because it's the great unknown. Let's face it - we all prefer certainty. Instead of becoming fixated on the 'fear of what could happen', we should express gratitude in our view of the future. How do we do this? Simply by maintaining hope, positivity and a growth mindset in relation to your attitude and outlook, you can rewire your brain to channel this disconcerting feeling of uncertainty into one of excitement for what's to come.

Gratitude - who knew it was that simple?

The Self-Sabotage of Happiness

Have you ever caught yourself thinking something along the lines of:

> I'LL BE HAPPY <u>WHEN</u> I GO ON HOLIDAY.

> I'LL BE HAPPY <u>WHEN</u> I GET THE NEW JOB/PROMOTION.

> I'LL BE HAPPY <u>WHEN</u> I GET THAT NEW CAR.

Happiness

The problem with this approach is that our happiness then becomes contingent upon something that is completely conditional. We're telling our Subconscious not to be happy unless and until something happens in the future.

What you end up doing here is foregoing all the potential happiness in the present by putting off your happiness until some future end state: an end state that is, by nature, not able to be reached in your present. You are sabotaging your own happiness by preventing yourself from experiencing it here and now. You then become focused on the achievement of this 'source of happiness' goal and overlook everything that you should be grateful for. I'm quite certain we can all relate to having worked hard to achieve something we thought would make us 'happy', only to realize shortly after that it hasn't changed anything. *What a let down.*

Instead of saying *'I will be happy when...'*, we should wake up each morning, reflect on everything we have to be happy for in the present and express gratitude for these – a roof over your head, supportive friends, a loving family, a diverse and inclusive work culture, hobbies that you love, aspirations for the future, hopes and dreams... You should be thankful for all the things that bring you joy in the present, as these are already in your life.

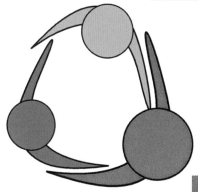

"LET US RISE UP AND BE THANKFUL,

for if we didn't learn a lot today,
at least we learned a little,
and if we didn't learn a little,
at least we didn't get sick,
and if we got sick,
at least we didn't die;

SO LET US ALL BE THANKFUL."

— BUDDHA

So what does being Grateful actually do?

Through simply expressing gratitude, happiness levels are shown to increase an average of 15%. Neuropsychologists have demonstrated that gratitude releases serotonin and also impacts cortisol levels in the brain. So, simply by expressing gratitude, you're able to manage your own stress levels. When you reflect on, or recall, past significant achievements, it allows the brain to re-live the experience. Since our Subconscious is unable to distinguish between what is reality and what is imagined, your brain releases serotonin and you feel happier as a result.

Gratitude reminds us that we're valued and have much to value in life. Research shows us that gratitude can help you become more forgiving, more satisfied with your life and less likely to have depressive thoughts or limiting self-talk. Expressing gratitude is a remarkably simple practice that enables us to receive incredible personal benefits. Expressing gratitude is something we can all easily and effortlessly commit to. If you find you're in need of a boost of happiness during a stressful day, just take a few moments to reflect on past achievements and victories, focus on something in your life that you're grateful for or just thank someone for being in your life. It's that easy.

IDEAS TO REMEMBER

1. An expression of gratitude is the simplest way to boost happiness. Focus on what you have to be thankful for now – health, happiness and life – and communicate to your Subconscious that you're happy. Don't sabotage your ability to be happy now by basing it on the condition of something that you want in the future.

2. Your Subconscious is the warehouse that stores all of your memories. Revisit any painful or negative memories to identify what they taught you and how they strengthened you. Forgiveness, both of people and experiences, is necessary for mental peace and wellbeing. In this way you can redefine your Subconscious 'wounds' into strengths and lessons that you can be thankful for.

3. Your future direction is in your mind, now. Figure out what you love to do – your cause, your purpose, your 'why' – then do it. Share your passion with others and be thankful for the motivation and inspiration it gives you.

4 Challenge FOUR

GRATITUDE

I want you to make gratitude a habit. Think of all the people, things, experiences and blessings you have in your life to be thankful for.

There are three things we're going to do going forward.

1. Keep a daily journal of three things you're thankful for. This works well first thing in the morning or just before bed. **This is going to become your Book of Gratitude.**

2. Make it a practice to tell a spouse, partner or friend something you appreciate about them every day.

3. Look in the mirror when brushing your teeth and think about something you've done well recently or something you're proud of.

Trust me, there will always be things you learn, ways you grow and things that broaden your perspective, and once you get into the habit of focusing on the positives and always be grateful for these, you'll find that you will become a much happier, more positive, more fulfilled person as a result.

NEGATIVE EXPERIENCE	WHY I'M GRATEFUL
Examples:	
I was certain I would get promoted at the end of last year but someone external was hired instead.	*I'm thankful to have had this experience as I learned to always be detached and not to place my sense of self worth on my work title. I know my worth and I'm stronger as a result.*
1.	
2.	
3.	

HACK V.

BE THE CHANGE

Help others and make a difference

> "Success isn't about how much money you make, **IT'S ABOUT THE DIFFERENCE YOU MAKE IN PEOPLE'S LIVES.**"
>
> – Michelle Obama

In movies, the 'good' characters – the ones that help others, save lives, restore peace and order – are typically the ones who end up experiencing good fortune. It's part of the Hollywood formula, and it's what audiences want to see. Surely you've heard the proverb, *'Good things happen to good people.'* 'Good' people are the ones who are kind-hearted, never harm others and generally possess an abundance of positive qualities in spite of often facing great challenges during their lives.

Remarkably, Neuroscience has shown when we perform acts of kindness it activates the pleasure center of our brain, which affects how we feel. Studies demonstrate that when people donate to charity, help others and perform acts of service, the mesolimbic pathway in the brain is triggered – this is the part of the brain responsible for feelings of reward and happiness. You know that warm, fuzzy feeling you get when you help someone? That's the one I'm talking about.

Your brain releases the feel-good chemical of oxytocin, which acts as encouragement to increase your generosity and makes you want to perform repeated acts of service. Oxytocin helps to enhance feelings of empathy and a desire to 'give back' – in fact, in one study that required participants to share money with a stranger, infusions of oxytocin were shown to increase by as much as 80% (details found in Zak, Stanton & Ahmadi's publication, called *Oxytocin Increases Generosity in Humans,* 2007). This is otherwise known by psychologists as 'a helper's high'. *That's why helping others feels so good!*

These acts of kindness could include the simplest of things. You could hold the door open for someone. You could offer to perform chores for other people. Perhaps just donating to charity, or even buying lunch for a friend as a gesture of gratitude. These seemingly simple actions, many of which don't require spending any money at all, can significantly increase your happiness and have the effect of attracting more positive things in your life.

Service makes us happy. Happiness makes us more positive. Positivity breeds positivity in others, which makes them happy, which makes us happy as the instigator of their happiness.

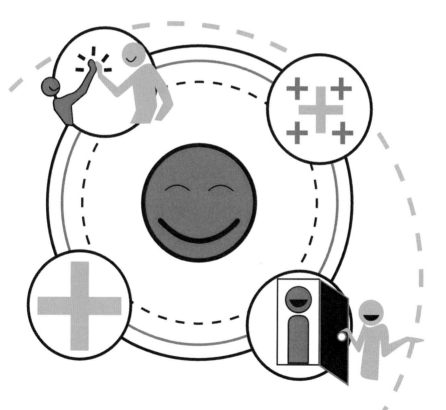

There you have it: **THE CYCLE OF BLISS.**

The Evidence

We know that giving to others 'feels good' for the giver because surely we've all felt it – that rewarding feeling we get when we know we're responsible for brightening someone's day or offering an act of kindness. Interestingly though, this has only recently been the subject of psychological research. In one 2005 publication on a study by Lyubomirsky, Sheldon & Schkade, participants were asked to perform a random act of kindness each day over a six-week period. Those who did experienced a significant increase in happiness as compared to control groups.

In a 2008 study conducted by Dunn, Aknin, & Norton, published in their article *Spending Money On Others Promotes Happiness*, participants were given either a $5 note or a $20 note to spend on others or donate to charity.

These participants experienced greater spikes in happiness compared with people given the same amount to spend on themselves.

The amount of money didn't even impact the level of happiness experienced; it was simply the act of giving it to someone else. Psychological evidence points to a virtuous circle of self-perpetuation. Happiness encourages us to give more. When we give more, we feel happier. This leads to a greater tendency to want to give, and the cycle continues.

The Benefits

People who volunteer and help others typically have a higher self-esteem, enhanced wellbeing and greater happiness than those who don't. As you now know, service to others triggers the release of certain chemicals in the brain that make you feel more connected to others, increases your confidence and gives you a greater feeling of empowerment. This increases your happiness levels and makes it easier to notice the things in your life for which you should express gratitude, and doing so makes you even happier. In a 2009 journal article by Pace, Neg Adame, Cole, Sivilli, Brown & Raison, the authors found that the power of helping others also reached as far as the body's immune and stress response systems.

Helping others has been shown to buffer the negative effects of naturally occurring stressors on emotional wellbeing by lowering brain cortisol levels, helping you feel calmer and more peaceful. So, next time you're feeling a little stressed, do something out of the norm. Take your mind away from the 'stressor stimulus' just for a moment and do something selfless for someone else. You may just find yourself instantly feeling a whole lot better, and you'll find it easier to be grateful for things in your life.

THANK YOU, HAPPY HORMONES!

Of course, the psychological benefits also depend on how often you perform acts of kindness and help others, as well as your underlying motivation. Why do you actually help people? Is it purely for your own benefit? Is it to be recognized? Is it because you feel forced to do so? It's only when we perform acts of kindness because we genuinely want to serve others, to give back, to help those less fortunate – this is when you experience the true positive psychological benefits.

Basically, the more regularly you help others and volunteer your time and efforts – and do so out of a genuine desire to create a better community and a better world – the more confidence you'll gain, the more positive you'll feel, the more gratitude you'll express and the happier you'll become. Naturally, you'll want to help more. It's a wonderful, self-perpetuating positive process, and we can all choose to be involved.

"To the world you may be just one person,
BUT TO ONE PERSON YOU COULD BE THE WORLD."

–Unknown

We should never think that we're insignificant – that we are only a single person with absolutely no influence. One single act of kindness today to a friend or stranger could influence so much more than we can imagine. Its influence may not even be felt or realized today – it may help that person when they need it most in the future. Going forward, whether you're explicitly asked or not, seek and create opportunities to help others when and how you can. You never know when a simple act of kindness will cause a long-lasting, positive ripple effect in the world. You may not feel it immediately, but as the ripples spread outward and impact others, they're likely to find their way back to you in surprising and wonderful ways. Even if they don't, you'll have the satisfaction of knowing you've helped another in an unqualified, selfless way.

"We make a living by what we get,
BUT WE MAKE A LIFE BY WHAT WE GIVE".

– Winston Churchill

IDEAS TO REMEMBER

1. Make a commitment to be of greater service to others. Seek out and create opportunities to offer acts of kindness where and how you can, no matter how large or small. The more you think about helping others, the more it becomes impressed upon your Subconscious, and you'll begin to act in ways that are of service without consciously having to think about it.

2. At the end of each day, take a moment of peaceful reflection, of quiet mindfulness, and bring yourself to account – ask yourself: *"Did I make the most of the opportunities I had today to make a difference in someone's life?"*

3. Next time you're experiencing stress, notice a self-limiting belief or pessimistic explanatory style, seek out opportunities to help others – volunteer your time, perform an act of kindness or help someone. It will have a profound impact on how you feel.

5 Challenge FIVE

Service to others

This is an easy one, and doesn't really require much, other than a commitment to being conscious about how we can help others, how we can serve them, and how we can offer random acts of kindness to anyone we meet.

At the end of each day, before you go to sleep, think back to all of the opportunities you had to make a difference in someone's life, no matter how large or small. Reflect on whether you took up the opportunity, or whether you let it pass.

For any you let slip, resolve to focus on these the following day so that you can be sure that every time an opportunity presents itself for you to help someone else, you make the most of it and take pride in knowing that you have 'done good' in the world.

"The best way to cheer
yourself is to try to
cheer someone else up."

– Mark Twain

CHAPTER FOUR

A Product,
Not A Prisoner

CHAPTER FOUR

A Product, Not A Prisoner

"We are products of our past,

BUT WE DON'T HAVE TO BE PRISONERS OF IT."

– Rick Warren

Now you understand that the way you perceive the world is through your own eyes. It's shaded by your experiences, your beliefs, your values, your upbringing, your environment, your opportunities, your struggles and your triumphs. It's influenced by your abilities, talents, skills and passions, aspirations, dreams and world-view. Our perception of the world around us is also influenced by a range of innate biological predispositions that we have little voluntary control over.

We know that we're a product of our past (and of course our genetic makeup). I've always believed that the world does, in fact, revolve around ME. **Before you jump to assumptions, let me explain.** My world is the world I see through my eyes, hear through my ears and make sense of through the workings of my mind. The way I perceive and interpret the world around me, what I see, hear, feel, smell and experience, is mine and mine alone. Similarly, the 'world' of my brother revolves around him. The 'world' of my best friend revolves around her. This is true also for every individual in every corner of the planet.

Where this becomes problematic is when people use this to justify bias, to justify prejudice, to justify selfishness and nihilism. Just because my world revolves around me doesn't exclude other people from having their own subjective experiences, views and perspectives. It also doesn't mean that by default I am always 'right'. In childhood, the understanding that other people 'see' the world differently, through their own eyes, is known as Theory of Mind.

THEORY OF MIND is the ability to attribute mental states - including beliefs, desires, intentions, thoughts & feelings - to oneself and others, and understanding that others have perspectives and experiences that are different to our own.

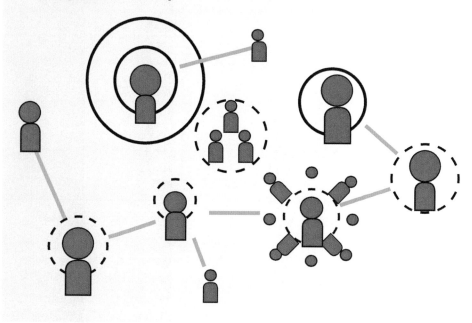

It's the most important social cognitive developmental milestone in early childhood, and something we should not forget as we journey through adulthood. Other people's perspectives matter too.

The Golden Rule

The Golden Rule… You all know it. You've all heard it. It asks you to *'treat others as you would like to be treated'.* It encourages generosity of spirit, respect, consideration, patience, kindness, love and pretty much every other human virtue.

I'd like to use this opportunity to submit for consideration a supporting Rule, one that is founded upon a friend's recent experience while working in Tokyo.

Ben was working as a very senior Management Consultant at a global company based in Japan. At the time, he was unmarried and had no children – a stranger to responsibility other than to perform in his role, which he did with ease.

Each Tuesday, Wednesday and Thursday night, he would take his team to the local karaoke bar, brimming with the energy of his youth, the pride of his professional success and the excitement that comes with the absence of any 'out of work' responsibility (not to mention his ability to 'party hard' with minimal consequences the following day, clearly another reflection of his youth). Ben loved staying out late, and I mean well into the following morning. He shared with me that he was astounded to find that his Japanese team members would stay out just as late as he would, despite majority being married with children.

When Ben noticed one or more of his team members displaying visible signs of fatigue, he felt that as their boss it was his duty to encourage them to return home. Yet, every time, they would all remain. So as not to appear pushy nor to be pressuring his team members, Ben left it, assuming they were having as much fun as he was.

It wasn't until quite some time after when a fellow expat commented to him in private that his team members were not 'culturally permitted' to leave until their boss left. They were not staying out of enjoyment, rather out of a sense of obligation and culturally engrained respect for their superior.

The moment Ben became aware of this he felt deflated. Not only had he been culturally insensitive, he now felt personally responsible for keeping these men away from their families in a culture where family is extremely important. Ben learned a valuable lesson about cultural norms and the dangers of making uninformed assumptions.

Treating others as we would like to be treated presupposes that every person sees the world through our eyes and interprets the world through the processing system of our mind. As we know, this is far from reality. This essentially denies Theory of Mind, and takes a 'me'-centric view of the world and the people within it. Let's take an example from the service industry. If I work in a customer service role, and I myself am totally content with average service, should I be delivering consistently average service to the customers I encounter? Or, as with Ben's example above, if I travel to a different country with a different culture, should I disregard any cultural norms and be blind to cultural sensitivities simply because I do not expect these for myself? While these may be extreme examples, they serve to illustrate the point.

I completely support the principle behind The Golden Rule and what it aims to achieve. To take this rule to another level, the additional rule I propose comes from Life, Business and Relationship coach Juan Calderon. He calls this: **The Platinum Rule**.

According to the Platinum Rule, we must start with the *other* person. Put *them* first. Put yourself in *their* shoes. Be truly selfless. Think of what *they* would like to receive and how *they* would like to receive it. Take yourself out of your reality and imagine viewing the world through *their* eyes. It requires an understanding of the person far beyond simply recognising their common humanity.

WHO ARE THEY?

WHERE HAVE THEY COME FROM?

HOW DID THEY GET HERE?

WHERE ARE THEY GOING?

What experiences have they been through that would shade the glasses of their perception and ultimately, their life?

The Platinum Rule has only a single word change, yet shifts the entire emphasis from internally focused to one that's external to ourselves. It shifts the focus to *them*.

THE PLATINUM RULE:

Treat others as THEY would like to be treated.

With one simple word substitution, we now have a Rule that has implied prerequisites. Empathy. Understanding. Selflessness. Awareness.

When you understand how others want be treated, then you are in the position to bring happiness to them, and in turn become happier yourself.

"Let no one ever come to you without leaving better and happier."

- Mother Teresa

CHAPTER FIVE

TAKE THE LEAD:
Bring it All to Life

TAKE THE LEAD:
Bringing it all to Life

Positivity in Action

If I had to think of one person in my life who is the embodiment of positivity, I know exactly who it would be.

When I used to work and live in Sydney I'd walk into my tall office building in the CBD, through the sterile automatic glass doors and across the minimalist lobby. Every day, without fail, I would be welcomed by the towering friendly giant who goes by the name of Gerry.

Gerry is a very tall Security Guard who just happens to be the most genuinely happy, smiley person I have ever – *and I mean ever* – come across. Keenly seeking the attention of the lifeless hordes of employees, Gerry would stand proudly at the entrance to the employee-only security gate that leads to the elevators. Each morning, Gerry would be seen wearing a beaming, sincere smile. The constant appearance of the upturned corners of his mouth and the creases at the sides of each eye attest to his perpetually jolly nature. What's more, any moments of shared eye contact would be celebrated by the most beautifully goofy wave and a resounding *'hello',* articulated in the overly rounded and drawn out sounds that are so typically Gerry.

Gerry's reputation for being the 'greeter of happiness' far precedes him. I initially heard about Gerry years ago in my first few months with the company when I worked at one of our smaller sites. An esteemed and deeply respected manager told me to *'look out for a guy called Gerry who guards head office.'* When I queried *'why?,'* I was advised, *'Gerry is just 'bout the happiest person you'll ever meet.'* This defining brand has become synonymous with this wonderful human.

On one of my last days in Sydney as I was leaving the building, I took a moment to stop and speak to Gerry beyond a fleeting greeting in passing.

"How are you today Gerry?" I asked.

"I'M AMAZING! AND HOW ARE YOU?"

"I'm great! Gerry, do you ever have a bad day?"

I was curious to find out whether this positively exemplary individual ever had moments as the rest of us do – moments where we are overcome with the stressors of life and the world seems too much.

"No room for a bad day. You've just got to smile through it."

Wow, this man really lives what he preaches.

"… And Gerry, is there anything in particular you repeat to yourself to stay so positive?" I was eager to discover his secrets.

'Not really. I just smile.' He flashed his sincere expression of pure joy once more. 'I smile because I'm happy. I'm happy because I smile. You see, if I don't smile, nobody else does. If nobody's smiling, what kind of a life is that? I smile so that they smile, and then their happiness makes me happy.'

This 60-second encounter and the words of simple yet profound wisdom left me a changed person. Gerry recognised his role in the happiness of others. He acknowledged the part he plays in bringing about the 'smiles' of others. He embodies what it means to center your life around Self. Gerry wouldn't let anyone affect his positivity; he is entirely focused on being the best he can be. He also, possibly unknowingly, was living proof of this wonderful phenomena called the *facial feedback loop*.

The Facial Feedback Loop

When we're happy, our brain releases neurochemicals that trigger a process that activates our facial muscles to smile. Smiling is the universal expression for happiness and joy. Just like how you smile when you're happy, you can actually make yourself happy simply by smiling. The reason why lies in neuroscience.

If you were to pick up a pen and grip it between your teeth, as a dog would do a bone, you would start to feel happier in as little as 30 seconds. This is because by forcing your facial muscles into a 'smile' shape, even if you're not remotely happy, you trigger the same part of the brain that releases hormones that make you happy. It's basic conditioning. You essentially 'trick' your brain into thinking you're experiencing joy.

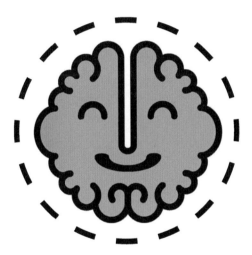

For starters, smiling activates the release of neuropeptides that have a part to play in reducing stress levels. Neuropeptides are small molecules used by neurons to communicate with each other. Neurons carry messages between the brain and body when we are happy, sad, stressed and excited. You also release the feel-good neurotransmitters of endorphins, dopamine and serotonin when you smile. This not only relaxes your entire body, but it can also lower your heart rate and blood pressure.

Think back to the last time you were unhappy. Perhaps you were sad, stressed, anxious, frustrated or angry. Whatever emotion you experienced, recall what happened to your face. Your lips may have become pursed, your jaw tense, and the muscles around your eyes may have tightened.

Negative emotions activate a physiological response that triggers different muscles in your face to tense. Your expression becomes almost the complete opposite of a 'smile', reinforcing how you feel. Interestingly, just by softening the tension and curling up the sides of your mouth, even if only into a 'fake smile' (or a non-Duchenne smile), you can actually trick yourself into feeling happier. Try it next time you're feeling down.

What happens to you when someone smiles? Do you smile back? Of course you do. This is a human response, a primed reaction to a stimulus. You may turn around to make sure this person has identified the correct 'target' of the smile, to make sure you're not hijacking the intended recipient (*I know we've all smiled back at someone, only to embarrassingly realise shortly after that they were smiling at someone else… awkward*). Generally though, your immediate first response is to reciprocate.

The part of your brain that's responsible for your facial expression when you smile, when you're happy or when you're mimicking another person's smile, resides in the cingulate cortex, an unconscious automatic response area. If someone asks you, *'How was your day?'* while they're smiling genuinely, you're more likely to respond positively than if they were to ask you the exact same question but with a negative tone devoid of a smile. We can induce certain responses simply by how we choose to ask a question or pose a statement. In the same way, our responses are influenced by the manner in which the other person engages us – the reasons lie with the brain.

GERRY UNDERSTOOD THIS.

He lived it.
He breathed it.

Gerry's demonstration of this concept was far more intentional than I had thought. His simple act of joyful connection, promoted by his genuine desire to spread happiness, was undoubtedly inspiring to the thousands each day who walked in and out of those sterile glass doors and just happened to catch Gerry's eyes. Where he smiled, they smiled. When they smiled, they became happier, even if only marginally. When they became happier, they became more positive. When they were more positive they were a step closer to experiencing the full ambit of benefits that come from positive thinking - greater confidence, greater resilience, less stress and more positivity in their lives.

The transformative power of a simple smile.

My Choice, My Responsibility:
PSYCHOLOGICAL OWNERSHIP

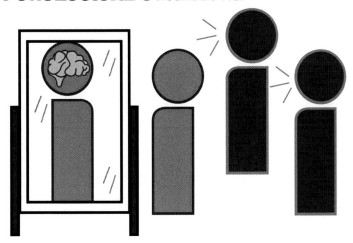

Jenny, an ambitious and driven colleague of mine, was at a crossroads in her working career. After four years of successfully working her way up the ranks of her organisation, she was looking for her next move. As a young professional with immense leadership potential, Jenny believed that the only way to progress her career was to take on a role as a leader, managing a team of people.

Her good fortune struck when a senior leader in another business area approached her with a promotion opportunity. While it was aligned with her short-term aspirations – those of people leadership – it wasn't in the area she'd hoped to get into. Jenny wanted to run a team in Operations, yet the role she was offered was in the Sales business: two very different business areas with very different priorities.

Unsure of whether she should accept the role or wait in her current position for her ideal role to become available, she sought the advice of others. She spoke to colleagues, friends, family and her partner. She even asked the elderly lady she sat next to on the train. The responses were varied, with some opportunists encouraging her to take the promotion and jump at the challenge. Others, more conservative in their approach, advised her to wait patiently for the role she really wanted.

The most influential person in her life, her partner, told her she would be foolish not to take the opportunity that was in front of her. Jenny took his advice and accepted the role.

It's now been four months since Jenny's decision to take on the role. Jenny has split from her partner and resigned from her company.

Wait... What?

WHY?

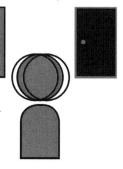

Well, here's what happened. Jenny signed the contract and started the role, eyes bright at the thought of greener pastures. She entered into it with the right attitude, with the right mindset and the approach of a winner. After all, she felt as though she had won.

Of course, that was short-lived. Three weeks later, the role of her dreams became available. This was the role she she actually wanted – the one she had been waiting for, the role that was perfectly aligned with her skills and strengths and the one that would catapult her career progression. Yet, it wasn't hers for the taking. She's taken the other role. Jenny had seventeen months and one week until her contract was complete. Now she felt as though she'd lost. Had she any indication of the possibility that the other role would become available there is no way she would have accepted her current position. She felt cheated.

Jenny became resentful of her partner who, after all, was the one whose advice she had taken. He was the one who encouraged her to accept the *wrong* position. Now she was stuck with it, while someone else – someone less qualified, someone less skilled, or worse, someone who didn't want it as much as she did – was offered the role that could have been hers. Jenny blamed her partner entirely. She felt powerless, as though she had lost control of her future. It was his fault. Why did she listen to him? Why did she accept his advice?

Her self-doubt and resentment made her despondent at work. She lost her passion and could no longer find her once so resolute motivation. As expected, she couldn't overlook the fact that it was her partner's advice that put her into this mess. Naturally, this blame meant their relationship ended rather abruptly, followed shortly after by her once-so-promising career at her company.

All this from a single choice.

Jenny's Cognitive Blind Spot

There's a psychological phenomenon involving something called a 'cognitive blind spot', which can make it difficult for us to honestly assess our actions and take ownership. This is what happened to Jenny. She made a decision, and then when she subjectively decided later that it was the 'wrong' decision, she placed the blame on her partner.

Our brains are hard-wired to flatter and shield our egos from blame when we make mistakes. What then happens is we find someone or something else to 'blame' to take the attention away from ourselves. People who shift blame to someone else further engage in irrational thinking in order to justify the blame. Jenny thought to herself,

> **"It's my partner's fault that I missed out on the job of my dreams because he was the one who told me to take the other position. He doesn't understand me or what I want in life."**

The more she focussed on these justifications, the more convinced she became of them, and this eventually led to their split.

'The moment you decide upon a course of action it becomes yours and yours alone.'

Some of us may find ourselves in a situation where, like Jenny, we make a decision that is founded upon someone else's advice or someone else's experience. If you find yourself relying solely on the advice and input of others, what you are really telling yourself is that your opinions and views don't matter.

You are valuing other people's opinions far above your own. You essentially disown yourself. Somewhere in your mind you are telling yourself that other people must know better.

We need to recognise that the moment we decide upon a course of action, it becomes ours and ours alone. No one knows the real you, but you. When you choose to make a decision, you must take full responsibility for both the decision itself and the consequences that result. When you realise this, it becomes incredibly empowering. This is what Jenny _didn't_ do. She blamed her partner wholeheartedly for her decision which led to great unhappiness.

While other people can influence a decision, they do not force you into action. You always make a choice. Blaming others means we transfer responsibility to them. Known as '**projection**', '**denial**' or '**displacement**', this sort of blame helps you preserve your sense of self-esteem by avoiding awareness of your own flaws or failings. In doing this, we avoid having to take ownership of the mistake (which may be more comfortable in the short-term), but it also denies us the opportunity to learn and grow from the experience.

I was able to work with Jenny to help her realise that she shouldn't be fearful of making mistakes. I helped her acknowledge that she is human and mistakes are part of life – they teach us lessons and help us grow. Armed with a growth mindset, we all need to learn to trust our best judgment, to own our decisions and to be committed and follow through. **No decision is ever the 'wrong' decision - it may simply be an opportunity to do better next time.**

"What you decide will never impact you as much as how you handle the consequences of making that decision"

– Michael Neill

CHAPTER SIX

THE SHADOW

The Shadow

Some time ago I applied to represent Australia at a preeminent leadership conference overseas. Of all applicants, ten delegates were to be selected for this incredible honour. I was quietly confident about my prospects – ok, I was pretty certain I'd be accepted – and had already planned my overseas holiday around the event. You know when you just have that feeling that you're going to be successful? Yup, that was me. I had it in the bag. I just knew it.

While I hadn't specifically told people I was going to the conference, I was openly sharing that I would be spending a week in the hosting city amidst my travel adventures. 'Create the Future you Want', 'Share Your Goals' and 'Program your Subconscious'. These are the concepts I believe in and share with others. This is exactly what I was doing.

Then, finally, I received a voicemail from the head of the selection panel, asking me to call her back about my application. It was time – I would finally have confirmation that I had been accepted and would be able to confirm my travel plans and book my flights. *At last!* I found a small empty room and hit redial.

The usual telephone etiquette ensued, and then this:

"Shadé, thank you for calling me back.

Firstly, we wanted to thank you for your application.

All applications we received were at an extremely high standard...

While we were deeply impressed with what you have done for the community and your contributions to the workplace, unfortunately you **WERE NOT** SUCCESSFUL..."

Radio silence.

Um... that was not what I was expecting. That was not what I had planned for. That was not what was meant to happen.

I felt a sense of mild nausea erupt from deep in my lower abdomen. For the first time in a while, I didn't know how to respond. My immediate reaction was simply to utter, 'Oh... um, that's ok...' I was overwhelmingly, devastatingly disappointed.

How did I get this so wrong? How did I mislead myself to such an extent that I was convinced that I'd be accepted?

Still holding the phone to my ear, I paced the small room. What was I meant to say now? How do I hide my disappointment? I forced myself to end the call with a positive note, thanking the message-giver for the call and promptly hanging up. Numbness.

Deflated and feeling completely rejected, I walked back to my desk. I sat in silence for some time, unsure what to do. I felt paralysed. The unexpected had crept up on me without any notice, and I didn't like how it felt.

My mind was racing – did I not include enough in my application? Am I not doing enough to differentiate myself as a community leader? Have I been focusing on the wrong things all this time? What if I'm just not good enough? Self-doubt took control of my thoughts and left me mentally debilitated.

I quickly texted my dad with the news. After what couldn't have been more than 40-seconds he texted back with the most powerful response:

...Life is full of surprises. The key to success is how quickly you recover from setbacks and move on. Someone else needed to go to this event...

HOW'S THAT FOR INSTANT PERSPECTIVE. THANKS, DAD.

During this experience, my brain registered a negative emotion, and I subsequently allowed that emotion to take over. I surrendered to it so easily. If it weren't for my dad's comments, I would have spiralled into self-limiting doubt and negativity. His comments not only opened my eyes to the reality of the situation, but it was exactly what I needed to hear to snap out of it. Life has a way of providing lessons when you need it most, of revealing a weak point and uncovering vulnerabilities. In my moment of despair, all my attention shifted focus inwards to how I was feeling. I was only thinking about myself – not once did I stop to consider what this opportunity would mean for the other ten delegates who would embark on this life-changing experience.

Life is not about what happens to you, but how you choose to respond. **'Someone else needed to go on this event.'** Someone else will grow, someone else will develop, someone else will be deeply positively influenced and will be able to create ripples of positive change in the community and workplace. This was the only thought that helped me.

When my expectation and the reality didn't meet in the middle, everything I thought I knew disappeared from sight. I surrendered to the negative emotion of disappointment that was taking over my body. I was physiologically responding to what was going on in my brain – I felt nauseous, the blood flushed from my face and my knees became unstable. I felt as though I lost control of my conscious mind. The doubt that consumed me was clearly the result of insecurity buried deep in my Subconscious – a black box of despair had been opened. I became lost in the negative, self-limiting thought process associated with Personalising and Catastrophising. It was astounding just how rapidly this negativity took control and how my conscious thoughts became consumed by it.

For me, it certainly was a lesson: a lesson that we are all on a journey and will all encounter experiences that take us by surprise. **"Life is what happens to you when you're busy making other plans."** No one is perfect. Even if you feel you've mastered the art of positivity and happiness, I guarantee that you'll encounter obstacles and problems that you'll need to address. We can never anticipate fully what life has in store for us – all we can hope for is that when life hits us hard we have the mental resources available to help us grow from the experience and recognise the lesson.

The easiest and most effective strategy to get you back on track if you find yourself, like I did, blocked by Subconscious obstacles is by practicing being present. So what does that mean?

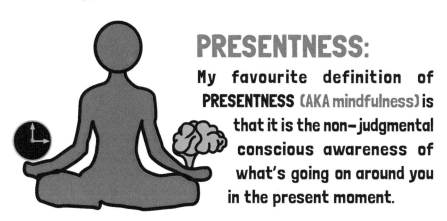

PRESENTNESS:

My favourite definition of PRESENTNESS (AKA mindfulness) **is that it is the non-judgmental conscious awareness of what's going on around you in the present moment.**

With genuine presentness you can return your focus to Self and turn negative emotions into your greatest strength. The steps on the next page outline what this could look like in practice. As with anything, the more you commit to being present and implement the following techniques, the easier it becomes and the quicker you'll be able to overcome challenges in the future. Again, it's a choice.

STEP 1. STOP:
Breathe

Once you become aware that your body has registered a negative emotion or feeling, **STOP**.
Take a deep breath, inhaling through your nose and exhaling through your mouth. Deep breathing increases the supply of oxygen to your brain and stimulates the parasympathetic nervous system to promote a state of inner calm. It's the most effective natural stress-buster. Don't inhibit what you're feeling. Similarly, don't ignore it or try to conquer it. Just allow it to 'be' and breathe through the experience.

STEP 2. IDENTIFY:
What do I feel?

Acknowledge that you've just received some 'data' from your body. It's trying to communicate something to you. Notice the emotion and how it's affecting your physiology. Recognise the feeling and whether you've felt it before. Is it familiar? Where do you feel it? Is it a feeling of tension? Of nausea? How is it manifesting itself physically in and on your body?

STEP 3. ACCEPT:
It is what it is

Don't deny what you feel. Accept what you're experiencing in the present. Through your mindful acceptance, you can embrace or hold the feeling in your awareness – this alone can have a calming effect. By accepting and embracing the negative emotion, you create a mental space around it and witness it instead of being consumed by it. This act of self-compassion is far more effective than denying the experience altogether. Through this, you'll soon feel that you are *not* your emotions. You're much larger than them.

PROBLEMS

NEGATIVITY

STEP 4. REALIZE:

It is Temporary

This step is about detachment. You need to realize and repeat to yourself that all emotions are impermanent and fleeting. They arise in response to a stimulus, linger, and then disappear. Your task here is to first acknowledge and then observe the emotion as it overtakes a part of your body, changes shape, and eventually dissipates. Instead of taking the negative emotion 'personally' and allowing it to deeply affect you, through mindfulness you're given an opportunity to view these emotions from a detached perspective, simply as psychological events, 'data points' that pass through – temporary waves in your ocean of awareness.

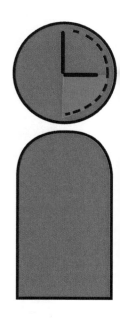

STEP 5. INVESTIGATE:

Locating the source

When you feel the emotion has passed, look deep into what you felt and try to understand what brought it on. What happened? What triggered it? Why did it cause such discomfort? You may find that you have particular values, beliefs, expectations or judgments about how you should behave or be viewed by others which has contributed to the onset of the emotion. Perhaps something brought back an unpleasant memory from your past. Allow the light of your presentness and awareness to help you gain insights into the source of the emotion.

TRUST YOURSELF:

You have the power

Trust yourself to choose the appropriate action – seek the lesson, the learning and the growth you can take from the experience. What did it teach you about yourself? What did you learn? Did you simply react to the emotion, or did you take time to respond? What was your explanatory style? Did you find yourself reverting to any lingering self-limiting beliefs? With this new awareness, what will you strive to do differently? It's important here that you redefine the experience as a life lesson and be grateful for what it's taught you. Gratitude in itself will give you strength and remind you that you're in control. You choose how you perceive and explain the world around you and the degree to which you recognise this will influence your future.

My personal experience with my perceived 'failure' of not being accepted into the program taught me so much about myself. It also shed light on my own areas of development and focussed my attention on improving myself. With the help of my dad's perspective, I was able to overcome this obstacle. Through the personal insights I gleaned from reflecting on my emotional reaction, I've been able to gain strength and know now that I'm better equipped should something similar catch me off-guard. You must believe that you too will be able to overcome anything you experience – you have the power to be the instigator of real change in your life.

Know it.   Believe it.   It's the truth.

CHAPTER SEVEN

CENTER ON SELF:
You are the
ARCHITECT

CHAPTER SEVEN

CENTERED ON SELF:
You are the
ARCHITECT

"I don't want to be Happy."

– SAID NO–ONE EVER

So there you have it. Now you know the basics for how you can become the Architect of your Life. The purpose of this book is to provide you with a glimpse into your Subconscious and its incredible power. It shows you just how easy it is to shift your attitude and explanatory style to be one of positivity and optimism and offers you the tools to become a happier individual… well, at least in theory.

Any journey begins with a single step, and the first step is always awareness. You can start by simply being aware of any self-limiting beliefs you have or any negative self-talk you engage in, and then take active steps to redirect your thoughts and behavior accordingly. You have the choice.

In light of everything covered in the preceding chapters, through the personal stories and the psychological theories, there are three Subconscious 'truths' that underscore our understanding of the mind. It's really important that you not only acknowledge but understand these so that you can implement everything you've learned.

THE FIRST TRUTH:

The Power of Now

The Subconscious Mind thinks only of the present. If any of your positive affirmations begin with *"I will…"* or *"I am going to…"* you're thinking in a future space. The Subconscious can't comprehend 'a future state' and therefore it won't have the impact you need it to. The key to making affirmations work and truly reprograming your Subconscious and your thoughts is to essentially 'trick' your Subconscious into believing you already have what you're seeking.

You need to expose your Subconscious to a desired future state, but phrase it as if you're experiencing it in the present. It needs to be framed in the 'now'. Positive affirmations should always be stated in the present; you want to feel as if you have what you want 'now'.

THE SECOND TRUTH:

There is no Difference

To the Subconscious Mind, there is no differentiation between what is real and what is imagined. Whatever you think or tell yourself, your Subconscious believes it to be true and works outside of your conscious awareness to prove that you're right. This is why visualisation is such an important technique in reprograming your beliefs and your thoughts – your Subconscious will accept it as reality and prime your thoughts and behavior towards attaining this goal.

The Subconscious is Illogical

Your conscious mind is characterized by rationality and is analytical by nature. By contrast, your Subconscious is illogical, irrational and non-analytical. The Subconscious makes no determination or judgment around the validity of information it receives or a belief you may have. It believes anything you tell it, regardless of whether it makes logical sense or not. It's designed simply to be the storage facility – the warehouse – to store whatever data is given to it, and this data can and will be accessed for later use. The Subconscious has no logical or rational reasoning capability. So, make sure you're aware of what you tell yourself or what beliefs you hold about your abilities (especially if they are self-limiting), and make them all positive and self-affirming.

Helen Keller once said, **if you *'keep your face to the sunshine…you cannot see shadow'.*** You have a choice here, and you need to choose to center your life on Self. You need to choose positivity, choose happiness, and choose to eliminate self-limiting beliefs and limiting language. You must choose to be grateful and serve others, and choose to be better than yesterday. No one can make this decision for you.

Your journey of personal growth is just that – it's yours and yours alone. As always, awareness is the first step, followed by ongoing commitment, perseverance and the unapologetic conviction of knowing that you'll be making a difference in your life, and importantly in the lives of others. It's certainly not easy, otherwise you already would've mastered the art of tapping into your Subconscious and there'd be no need for this book. But, if you tell yourself *"this is going to be so hard"* or *"I can't do it"*, then you've already sabotaged yourse I've even before you've begun.

The journey of a thousand miles starts with a single step. Reading this book has been your first step. It's up to you now whether you *choose* to take the next step, and which direction you *choose* to go. Equipped with these basic tools, you're empowered to center your life on Self, to focus your attention on how you respond to the world around you and ultimately become the Architect of the Life you want to lead. Because, guess what?

You already are.

The Future Is What You Design It To Be.

· ·

You Have The Power To Change The Way You Live.

· ·

Choose Positivity.
Choose Happiness.

· ·

You Are The Architect.

· ·

The Choice Is Yours.

"Yesterday I
was clever,
so I wanted
to change
the world.

Today I am
wise, so I
am changing
myself."

– Rumi

EXTRAS

EXAMPLE AFFIRMATIONS

I can find
something positive

in even the most
difficult situations.

I remind myself to

focus

on the
good things
in my life.

I PERSEVERE

no matter how
tough things get.

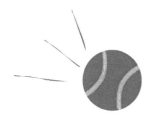

I Believe
that
I can
deal with
whatever
life
throws at me.

By allowing myself
to be happy,

I inspire others to
be happy as well.

I feel powerful, capable, confident, energetic and on top of the world.

I am grounded in my experience of the present moment.

I TRUST MYSELF
and know my
inner wisdom is
my best guide.

REFERENCES

"Because opinions without considering the facts are just plain dumb."

- Shadé's 'inappropriate' husband

REFERENCES

Office of Economic Cooperation and Development. (2015) The ABC of Gender Equality in Education: Aptitude, Behavior, Confidence. OECD Publishing.

Dunn, EW., Aknin, LB. & Norton, MI. (2008) Spending Money On Others Promotes Happiness. Science 319, 5870: 1687–1688.

Emmons, RA., & McCullough, M. E. (2003) Counting Blessings Versus Burdens: Experimental Studies of Gratitude and Subjective Well-being in Daily Life. Journal of Personality and Social Psychology, 84(2): 377-389.

Fredrikson, B. (1988) What Good Are Positive Emotions? (1988) Rev Gen Psychol, 2(3): 300–319.

Lyubomirsky S., Sheldon, K. & Schkade. (2005) Pursuing Happiness: The Architecture Of Sustainable Change. Review of General Psychology, 9(2): 111-131.

Pace, TW., Neg, LT., Adame, DD., Cole, SP., Sivilli, TI., Brown, TD. & Raison, CL. (2009) Effect Of Compassion Meditation On Neuroendocrine, Innate Immune And Behavioral Responses To Psychosocial Stress. Psychoneuroendocrinology, 34(1):87-98.

Seligman, MEP. (2002) Authentic Happiness: Using the New Positive Psychology to Realize Your Potential for Lasting Fulfillment. New York: Free Press.

Seligman, MEP. (1991) Learned Optimism. New York: Knopf.

Zak, PJ., Stanton, AA., Ahmadi, S. (2007) Oxytocin Increases Generosity in Humans. PLoS ONE 2(11): e1128.

Thank You!

To the reader,

Thank you so much for picking up this book and supporting this happiness movement. Also, thank you for investing in you – in your success, in your fulfillment and in your happiness.

I'd love to know how you found this book;
Do you have your own experience with discovering happiness? Have you been on the other side? Have you been able to implement any of the hacks?

I'd love to read your stories!

Jump onto the website **www.shadezahrai.com/contact** and leave your comments and feedback.

Can't wait to hear from you!

Yours in happiness,

Shadé

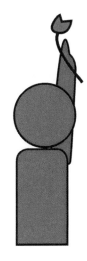

About the Author

Shadé Zahrai is an author, consultant, former lawyer, trainer, speaker, Future Leader Scholar (through the Westpac Bicentennial Foundation) and Australian champion Latin dancer & performer featured on TED. Shadé specializes in translating brain science research into simple, actionable strategies for performance and wellbeing. She is passionate about empowering women and minorities to challenge unconscious bias, drive inclusion and advance equality in the workplace and our communities.

Her mission is to help make the world a better place
- One happy person at a time.

For more information, visit: shadezahrai.com